KENT
STEAM

Scenes from the Fifties and Sixties

MICHAEL WELCH

Capital Transport

CONTENTS

Front cover A splendidly turned-out locomotive scoured and polished to perfection, an eye-catching headboard, huge arrows on the front and sides of the engine, the national flags of Great Britain and France and a beautiful rake of absolutely immaculate Pullman cars. . . there was no mistaking the colourful and distinctive 'Golden Arrow'! The down working is depicted between Beckenham Junction and Shortlands behind Bulleid Pacific No.34104 *Bere Alston. Ken Wightman*

Back cover No building is more closely identified with the Kentish landscape than the familiar oast house, or locomotive more associated, at least in latter years, with Kentish branch lines than an H Class. In this illustration SECR H Class 0-4-4T No.31177 is seen pulling in to Horsmonden station with a Hawkhurst-bound branch train on 2nd June 1961, just a couple of weeks prior to the line's demise. Strangely, this was the only picture submitted to the author that included an oast house in close proximity. Perhaps farmers in times past suspected that the polluting smoke and steam from passing engines might ruin the flavour of the hops, and persuaded the railway companies to steer clear of their land. On the other hand, most steam aficionados would probably have been delighted by the distinctive flavour of the resultant 'Locomotive Ale', which would no doubt have found a substantial niche market. So this gem of a picture portrays a rare combination, but what a pity the engine is so dirty. *David Clark*

Overleaf The SECR L Class 4-4-0s were part of the railway scene in Kent for well over 40 years and were popular and competent machines. In this evocative portrait, taken in beautiful low autumn sunshine in October 1957, No.31763 is seen leaving Tonbridge in charge of a 'Birdcage' set of coaches in red livery. During their heyday the Ls were rostered to work the fast Charing Cross to Folkestone expresses, but by the time of this picture they had been relegated to less exacting duties. Built in August 1914, No.31763 lasted until April 1960, so it certainly stood the all-important test of time. Each locomotive reportedly cost £4,195, hardly a fortune by today's values, so the locomotives' owners certainly seem to have got a bargain. One wonders whether each engine came with its own written guarantee! *Ken Wightman*

First published 2002

ISBN 185414 261 5

Published by Capital Transport Publishing,
38 Long Elmes, Harrow Weald, Middlesex

Printed by CS Graphics, Singapore

© Michael Welch 2002

INTRODUCTION

The white cliffs of Dover, oast houses, hop gardens and apple orchards are all enduring symbols of Kent, one of England's best-loved counties. It can justifiably boast one of the most attractive and varied landscapes, from the scenic North Downs to the wide open vistas of Romney Marsh. While these features undoubtedly dominate an outsider's view of the county, Kent also has some fine Victorian seaside resorts which were undoubtedly boosted by the coming of the railways. They have been popular with generations of visitors and Londoners in particular, though sadly in recent years they have declined as more Britons take their holidays abroad. It must be said, however, that Kent is not all idyllic pastoral landscapes and memorable coastline. In stark contrast to its 'garden of England' image, much of the county's north-west corner is heavily industrialised with mile after mile of drab factory estates and urban sprawl which make this part of the county indistinguishable from south-east London. Until relatively recently there was a thriving coal industry in eastern Kent, with its associated pithead gear and vast waste tips which marred the countryside for miles around. At one time an overhead aerial ropeway conveyed coal from Tilmanstone colliery to Dover for shipment, this being the type of installation more associated with the industrial north of England!

Railway development in Kent began as early as 1830 when the historic Canterbury & Whitstable Railway was opened for passenger and freight traffic, powered by steam. It was a short line, only six miles long, and served purely local needs, but its place in the history of railway development in southern England is assured. It was built primarily to transport goods from Canterbury to the north coast fishing town of Whitstable where a small harbour was developed. The River Stour had previously been used for this purpose, but it had been silting up since the days of King Henry VIII and little had been done to improve the river. The Canterbury & Whitstable Railway was incorporated by an Act of Parliament on 10th June 1825 and opened on 3rd May 1830 amidst great celebration and rejoicing. The line remained open for passengers until 1st January 1931 and was closed completely on 28th February 1953.

The history of main line railways in Kent is dominated by the South Eastern Railway (SER) and the London, Chatham & Dover Railway (LCDR) and today's system was largely shaped by these companies. The former had the greatest impact in the early years and obtained an Act of Incorporation on 21st June 1836 to construct a main line from London to Dover. Parliament insisted that only one line into the Capital from the south and south-east was necessary, so consequently a junction with the London to Brighton line was sanctioned at Earlswood Common, near Redhill. Trains were running as far as Tonbridge by 26th May 1842 and the route had reached Ashford by 1st December 1842. Many of the SER's wayside stations were characterised by their cheap construction with simple single-storey wooden clapboard buildings, staggered platforms and foot crossings across the line rather than footbridges. Services to Dover started running on 7th February 1844. The journey from London to Dover via Redhill was speeded-up when the Sevenoaks cut-off was opened in 1868.

The LCDR had as its foundation the East Kent Railway's 48½ miles long line from Strood to Canterbury, which received the Royal Assent in August 1853. This was essentially a locally-based landowners' line, which grew in a piecemeal fashion over a period of years. The East Kent had access to the SER's Strood station, and the all-powerful SER gave an undertaking not to oppose an extension of this fledgling railway company to Dover, which later turned out to be a serious miscalculation. The line from Strood to Faversham was opened throughout in March 1858, using locomotives borrowed from the Great Northern Railway! The rival SER was doubtless confident that the East Kent company would overreach itself and no doubt anticipated the onset of bankruptcy but, contrary to the SER's expectations, the company grew in strength and on 1st August 1859 changed its name to the London, Chatham & Dover Railway. Lack of funds prevented an immediate extension to Canterbury, but this was eventually opened on 9th July 1860. In 1858 the LCDR had obtained powers for an independent route (opened in December 1860) from Strood to St Mary Cray, where it connected with the Mid-Kent Railway, which gave the LCDR access to Victoria. Using powers obtained some years earlier, the LCDR reached Dover on 22nd July 1861, thus enabling the operation of a London to Dover service to challenge the supremacy of the mighty SER.

Steam traction was 'king' in Kent for more than 130 years and a few workings survived in the county far later than is commonly supposed. Regular steam working was eliminated from many parts of Kent when Phase One of the Kent Coast Electrification Scheme was inaugurated in June 1959 and Phase Two almost exactly two years later. The 9.30am Victoria to Dover boat train was still, apparently, steam-hauled down the Chatham Line as late as February 1961, No.34100 *Appledore* being recorded on the 4th of that month. The final South Eastern steam duty from a London terminal was the 5.45am London Bridge to Hastings, which was steam-powered until the end of the summer 1961 timetable. During periods of very bad weather steam sometimes deputised for electric traction, a notable example being on New Year's Day 1962 when *Appledore* (again!) was piloted by N Class No.31412 on the up 'Night Ferry'. A few steam duties lasted on the Tonbridge to Maidstone West/Hastings services until at least May 1962, while Tunbridge Wells West shed retained its steam complement until closure as an independent shed on 9th September 1963. Steam continued to power some rush-hour trains from the latter location to Eastbourne and Three Bridges until June 1965, but the engines were based at Redhill. The very last pocket of steam was at Ashford Works where USA Class 0-6-0T shunters worked until 10th July 1967 and there was a even a report that a C Class engine was still being used for supplying steam for axlebox cleaning a fortnight later – two weeks after the 'official' end of Southern Region steam. Could it be that Kent, besides having some of the first steam engines in the south of England, also had the last?

It has been great fun, and extremely satisfying, compiling this album and I would like to thank all of the photographers who have so kindly trusted me with their irreplaceable transparencies. In addition Terence Barry, Chris Evans, Dave Fakes and Graham Mallinson have read the proof and suggested many alterations and improvements which, I am sure, have vastly improved the final result.

A special 'thank you' is also due to David Clark and Fred Collins for the use of some magnificent images from the collection of the late Ken Wightman.

Burgess Hill, December 2001   Michael Welch

CHISLEHURST TO TONBRIDGE

One of the most interesting workings which served Kent during the twilight of the steam era was the 7.24am train from London Bridge to Ramsgate via Ashford. This remained a regular duty for a SECR 4-4-0 until the end of steam and consequently was heavily patronised by enthusiasts despite the early morning start. The train also drew many photographers and in this illustration D1 Class No.31739 is depicted passing Chislehurst on 1st June 1961, the station being visible in the background. *Paul Leavens*

The famous 'Golden Arrow' Pullman car train linked London with Paris and this train is seen here in all its splendour approaching Petts Wood on 16th May 1959. Motive power is provided by Bulleid 'Battle of Britain' Class Pacific No.34085 *501 Squadron*. Stewarts Lane shed always made a special effort to ensure that the locomotive rostered to work the 'Arrow' was turned out in magnificent condition, and No.34085 appears to be polished to perfection. The train is coming off a newly remodelled spur from Bickley Junction, on the former LCDR route, to Petts Wood Junction, on the former South Eastern Railway (SER) main line. The four-track SER line is just out of sight on the left of the shot. The untidy earthworks on the right are the remains of the old spur. During 1958/59 this area was the scene of a massive civil engineering operation to re-align various junctions and spur lines in order to relax the many speed restrictions, the speed limit on the section seen here being raised from 30 to 50mph. The extensive track work was spread over a long period and carried out during weekend possessions. Interestingly, the track was assembled in the layout yard at New Cross Gate prior to installation and as many as twelve trains would often be needed to convey the materials to the site. *David Clark*

The SER line from London has been steadily gaining height all of the way from New Cross, but after Orpington it steepens markedly, and climbs on a gradient of 1 in 120 until the summit is reached just after Knockholt station. The line then descends through Polhill tunnel on a gradient of 1 in 143, and in this shot the 7.24am London Bridge to Ramsgate working, with D1 Class No.31749 in charge, is pictured coasting downhill. In times gone by the signalmen at Polhill Intermediate box must have witnessed many spectacular fireworks displays as overburdened locomotives struggled past with heavy London-bound trains in tow. This picture was taken in May 1961. *Paul Leavens*

The 7.24am *ex*-London Bridge is seen once again, this time negotiating the junction with the route from Swanley immediately north of Sevenoaks station, also on a sunny May morning in 1961. The 7.24am certainly seems to have been a popular train! On this occasion E1 Class 4-4-0 No.31507 is in charge. This picture provides a panoramic view of the track layout, the old and new signal boxes and the distant North Downs. In the background of this busy scene, on the right of the picture, C Class 0-6-0 No.31244 waits with the empty stock of the 8.21am to Tunbridge Wells West, while a partially visible BR Standard tank locomotive 'blows off' in the foreground. The station here, formerly known as Sevenoaks (Tubs Hill), was reached by electrification as long ago as 1935, when a regular interval electric service to the Capital replaced the much less frequent steam stopping trains. Sevenoaks remained the terminating point for electric traction for over 25 years. South of the station a long damp cutting leads to Sevenoaks tunnel (3,451 yds), the longest on the former Southern Region. *Paul Leavens*

A pair of SECR L Class 4-4-0s, Nos.31764 and 31766, wait in the sidings just west of Tonbridge station with the empty stock of a train to Ashford, sometime in the late 1950s. In the foreground the very tightly-curved tracks of the main London to Dover line can be seen. The lines here have been realigned several times in order to ease the very severe permanent speed restriction at this point. The junction with the line from Redhill, which was the main route from London to Dover until the Sevenoaks cut-off was opened in 1868, is immediately behind the photographer. Designed in 1913 by Harry Wainwright, the L Class was intended to meet the need for more powerful motive power, within the weight constraints imposed by the Civil Engineer. Even so, the modestly proportioned L Class was not permitted to operate on the Chatham Section until Southern Railway days. Twenty-two engines were built by private contractors, including ten which were constructed and partially assembled in Germany by A. Borsig of Berlin. During World War I the Ls competently handled the heavy troop specials between the Channel ports and London. Withdrawals, which commenced in 1956, gathered pace when electric traction replaced steam on many Kentish lines and the last survivor, No.31768, was withdrawn in December 1961. *Ken Wightman*

When Bulleid Pacifics became available on the South Eastern Section after the war there was pressure on the operating authorities to restore 1939 express schedules, including the resumption of the 80 minute Charing Cross to Folkestone Central timing. An 85 minute schedule was introduced as early as 1946, but it was June 1953 before the 9.40am Margate to Charing Cross and 4.15pm return train were booked to run between Folkestone and London in 80min. The title 'Man of Kent' was bestowed upon these services, these being the last SR steam-operated trains to be named. In June 1956 another pair of trains was given the same title, in rather bizarre circumstances, as a result of the introduction of new BR Standard rolling stock, which replaced the Bulleid coaches previously employed. The latter vehicles had their carriage nameboards on the roof, so after the arrival of the up working at Charing Cross a railwayman had simply to walk along the roof to reverse the boards to ensure the 'Man of Kent' title was not displayed on the coaches, which were booked to form the 1.15pm departure to Margate via Dover. The Mk1 stock, however, followed LMSR practice and had their boards at cantrail level, just below the guttering. The up train used Platform Six at Charing Cross where there was no staging available on one side of the train, so it was not possible to change the boards. Thus the 1.15pm regularly passed the Waterloo headquarters offices displaying an unofficial title on one side of the coaches. Apart from partially rebuilding Charing Cross station(!), the problem was not easily solved, so it was decided to name both of the balancing workings, the 1.15 down and 12.40pm up from Margate. Eleven carriages was the customary formation, consisting of a 7-set, a corridor second vehicle plus a 3-set; the latter did not work beyond Dover. Power was normally a Bulleid Pacific or sometimes a 'Schools' 4-4-0, and in this shot No.34078 *222 Squadron* is seen easing its way around the curve west of Tonbridge with the 1.15pm *ex*-Charing Cross in June 1960, a year before the 'Man of Kent' disappeared from the timetable as a result of electrification. *Colour-Rail*

This absolute gem of a photograph is of considerable historical interest. SECR L Class 4-4-0 No.31767, looking superb in lined malachite green livery, is depicted at Tonbridge in the early 1950s. The repainting of these engines in this livery was sanctioned in mid-1946 and eventually the majority of the class was similarly treated, apart from six locomotives. Lined black became the standard colour after nationalisation, but it was not until June 1954 that the last example, No.31780, was repainted so this picture was presumably taken prior to that date. No.31767 was among the first of the class to be condemned, an event that occurred in October 1958. *Neil Davenport*

In this fine portrait Maunsell 'Schools' Class 4-4-0 No.30930 *Radley* is seen at Tonbridge in the late 1950s. This class was associated with the Eastern Section for over 30 years, but No.30930 actually began life at Fratton shed in December 1934, working Portsmouth to Waterloo expresses over the sinuous and heavily-graded Portsmouth Direct line. After this route was converted to electric operation in 1937, *Radley* moved to Bournemouth, again for use on London trains. In 1942 a reshuffle of motive power caused No.30930 to be transferred to Basingstoke, a move which occasionally resulted in its appearance at Exeter on a working from Salisbury, but the end of hostilities found it back at Bournemouth. After the war *Radley* was repainted in malachite green and was one of three machines moved to Brighton for working the cross-country trains from there to Bournemouth, Plymouth and Cardiff. By 1949 No.30930 had become firmly established on the Eastern Section, based at Bricklayers Arms shed for Kent Coast and Hastings line duties. Following a change of policy it was repainted black, but later carried Brunswick green after a further policy shift in 1956. *Radley* later migrated to the Central Section again, and was officially allocated to Brighton shed when withdrawn, with all of its remaining sister locomotives, at the end of 1962. Its official final mileage was 1,096,856. *Neil Davenport*

Photographed from a spot adjacent to Tonbridge motive power depot, Maunsell 'Schools' Class 4-4-0 No.30918 *Hurstpierpoint* coasts towards the station with an unidentified inter-regional train. Judging by the rolling stock, the train was probably heading for somewhere on the London Midland Region. Tonbridge, known as 'Tunbridge' for a time and then 'Tonbridge Junction' until 1929, has been an important centre for traffic from the earliest days of railways in Kent. Main lines radiate from the town to London, Redhill, Ashford and Hastings. The first line to serve Tonbridge was that from Redhill, which opened on 31st May 1842, this being extended to Ashford in stages, the latter town being reached on 1st December 1842. A short branch to Tunbridge Wells opened for business on 20th September 1845: this was also extended in stages, services through to Hastings starting in February 1852. The final line to reach Tonbridge was the route from Sevenoaks which opened in 1868. Known as the Sevenoaks cut-off, this reduced the distance between London and Dover by $12\frac{1}{2}$ miles and replaced the route via Redhill as the South Eastern Railway's trunk line to the Channel ports. *Ken Wightman*

A smartly turned-out L Class 4-4-0, No.31762, poses on Tonbridge shed in the late 1950s. The rather cramped motive power depot stood in the 'vee' of the Ashford and Hastings lines east of the station, the main building having three through roads. The allocation of Tonbridge shed remained remarkably unchanged over many years, the principal classes being SECR C Class 0-6-0s and H Class 0-4-4Ts supplemented by around a dozen 4-4-0s, also of SECR origin. A later development was the allocation of a sizeable batch of Bulleid Q1s to Tonbridge after World War II, these being employed on heavy freight trains between the various marshalling yards in Kent and neighbouring areas. Tonbridge is understood to have been the last location in Kent where BR steam engines could be observed, albeit not in use. This came about purely by chance when two American-built USA Class 0-6-0Ts, Nos. DS237 *Maunsell* and DS238 *Wainwright*, were 'stopped' with hot boxes whilst on their way from Ashford Works, where they had been employed as shunters, to South Wales for scrapping. The locomotives were dumped at Tonbridge shed for some months until purchased for further use on the preserved Kent & East Sussex Railway. *Ken Wightman*

The rugged and extremely powerful Bulleid Q1 Class 0-6-0s were, as previously stated, a familiar sight on freight work in Kent after World War II. They were quite versatile locomotives, however, and could sometimes be found on passenger duties. In this shot No.33035 is seen near Tudeley, between Tonbridge and Paddock Wood, hauling the 6.05am Reading South to Margate train in June 1961. The Q1 would have taken over the train after reversal at Redhill. The countryside along the 25 miles-long, straight section of line from Tonbridge to Ashford, through the Weald of Kent, is dominated by fruit farms and hop gardens. *Paul Leavens*

TONBRIDGE TO DOVER

Photographed during the last days of regular steam operation on the London to Dover main line, the evening sun glints on No.34012 *Launceston* as it gallops through Paddock Wood on the down through track with the 6.21pm Charing Cross to Ramsgate train on 8th June 1961. The station here, once known as 'Maidstone Road', has been a junction since the secondary line to Maidstone West opened in 1844 and the picturesque Hawkhurst branch opened throughout in September 1893. Paddock Wood was well-known for its stilted signal box, under which the Hawkhurst trains passed, and the handling of considerable amounts of farm produce, so it was quite a busy station. *Cliff Woodhead*

The 2.30pm Victoria to Folkestone boat train, headed by Bulleid 'West Country' Class Pacific No.34092 *City of Wells*, is depicted on the western outskirts of Ashford on 28th May 1961. Part of the sidings serving Chart Leacon electric depot are just discernible on the extreme left of the picture. No.34092, which was a regular sight on the Eastern Section for many years, was made redundant by electrification, and in May 1961 moved, together with three other Stewarts Lane engines, to Salisbury shed on the Western Section. In November 1962 it was one of the last unrebuilt Bulleid Pacifics to be granted a heavy repair at Eastleigh Works. Even this did not ensure its survival for long however, and No.34092 was withdrawn exactly two years later and sent to Barry scrap yard in South Wales. It was later rescued for preservation on the Keighley & Worth Valley Railway in Yorkshire and subsequently returned to main line use. It is currently undergoing a thorough, and no doubt extremely expensive, overhaul before returning for further main line operation. *Paul Leavens*

The fireman is at work moving the coal forward in the tender of D1 Class 4-4-0 No.31489 during its stop at Ashford station on 14th May 1960. The locomotive was powering the 7.24am London Bridge to Ramsgate train. Ashford, a major junction where secondary routes from Maidstone, Ramsgate and Hastings join the London to Dover main line, is probably best known as home to the locomotive works which was developed by the SER. The works opened in 1847 following a decision to move from New Cross and a site covering 185 acres was acquired – the much cheaper cost of land at Ashford compared to south London no doubt being a major factor. In 1850 a carriage and wagon works was also constructed. The works' employees, who numbered 3,000 at their peak, were housed in a 'railway town', located adjacent to the works, which was laid out around a central green. This settlement was largely self-contained and included a bath house, shop, public house and school, in addition to a Mechanics Institute. Perhaps the greatest days of Ashford Works were during the era of Harry S. Wainwright, who was Locomotive Superintendent from 1898 to 1913. During his period in office some classic designs appeared, the D Class 4-4-0s being arguably one of the most handsome and graceful steam locomotives ever to see the light of day. An imaginative new livery of Brunswick green (lined out with light green, yellow and red), black and vermilion with dark red underframes replaced the drab black livery favoured by his predecessor. Carriage production ceased soon after the formation of the Southern Railway in 1923, but locomotive and wagon building continued. During the 1920s/30s Ashford's major contribution towards the locomotive construction programme was the building of the Maunsell 'Moguls' and W Class 2-6-4Ts. During World War II, a small number of Stanier-designed 8F Class 2-8-0s were built for use overseas. No complete engines were constructed after nationalisation, but repair work continued to flourish, and even lasted into the early 1960s on a reduced scale. At this time Ashford became the graveyard for many engines, including such celebrated classes as 'Lord Nelsons', 'King Arthurs' and 'Schools'. The works continued to build and repair wagons for some years after the end of main-line steam working in Kent and steam traction remained in use for shunting duties. Three long-lived Wainwright C Class 0-6-0s were employed until 1965, when they were superseded by a pair of USA Class 0-6-0Ts displaced from Southampton Docks. The latter survived until 1967, becoming the last active BR steam locomotives in Kent. Some railway work, mainly the repair of cranes and wheels, continues on the site, but most of the works is now an industrial estate. *R.C. Riley*

Maunsell 'Schools' Class 4-4-0 No.30929 *Malvern* poses in the down main platform at Ashford after arrival with the 11.46am train from Charing Cross, sometime in the early 1960s. This was a semi-fast train which called at principal stations *en route* and reached Ashford, where it terminated, at 1.53pm. Built at Eastleigh Works in July 1934, No.30929 was amongst the final batch of 'Schools' Class engines withdrawn from traffic in December 1962. *Dennis Ovenden*

It would be a considerable understatement to say that Ashford station has changed since this picture of N Class No.31820, on the 2pm Tonbridge to Ashford 'all stations' train, was taken on 27th May 1961. The station was rebuilt in the early 1960s as part of the Kent Coast Electrification Scheme, when the old SER premises were swept away and replaced by rather stark, characterless buildings typical of that period. At least the replacement of Beaver Road overbridge at the western end of the station, which consisted of separate brick arches over each of the four running lines, enabled the station's two bay platforms to be converted into loops, thus greatly improving operational flexibility. The track layout was, of course, completely revised at that time, and the existing four mechanical signal boxes in the immediate Ashford area were eliminated, together with some rural ones, when a new panel box came into use in April 1962. Further signalling alterations occurred during the mid-1980s. The station was again reconstructed, and additional platforms provided, in the 1990s in connection with the introduction of Eurostar services to the continent. *Alan Chandler*

The unpretentious exterior of Folkestone Junction station is seen in this picture, which was taken on 22nd July 1962. The station here, which opened in December 1843 when the line was extended from Ashford, was the first permanent station to serve the town. Like many SER stations outside London it had staggered platforms, but was probably more famous for the numerous changes of name it suffered over the years. At first it was known simply as 'Folkestone', but the suffix 'Junction' was added in 1852. Between 1884 and 1897 its name reverted to 'Folkestone' once again, after which the 'Junction' suffix was used once more! From 10th September 1962 the premises were called 'Folkestone East', but this name was short-lived, because the station was closed from 6th September 1965. At least the station had one dubious claim to fame – it was the first British junction station seen by countless travellers from the continent! *Michael Allen*

A panoramic view of the layout at Folkestone Junction, looking eastwards from the station footbridge. The down platform is prominent on the left, with the roof of the three-road engine shed visible on the extreme left of the photograph. The depot was actually a sub-shed of Dover where a handful of R1 Class 0-6-0Ts, and latterly GWR pannier tank locomotives, were based for working the harbour branch, and larger locomotives were turned and serviced between boat train duties. The 532 yards-long Martello Tunnel, named after the tower above it, is discernible in the far distance. On the right of the main line, in the middle distance, are three sidings where boat trains to and from the harbour reversed. In the foreground is Bulleid 'Battle of Britain' Pacific No.34068 *Kenley* which appears to be waiting to take over a boat train bound for London. To the right of the locomotive are carriage sidings and, out of view, the goods yard.
P. J. Kelly/Colour-Rail

In this further view at Folkestone Junction, taken looking across the main line tracks from the carriage sidings, two locomotives can be seen in the shed yard. The one nearest to the photographer is R1 Class 0-6-0T No.31107 which was one of 25 engines of the class designed by James Stirling, and built at the South Eastern Railway's Ashford Works between 1888 and 1898. The locomotives were originally constructed as R Class, but 13 were later rebuilt by Wainwright and reclassified R1. It is recorded that No.31107 was sub-shedded at Folkestone Junction as long ago as 1937 and was still based there in July 1953. When this shot was taken, on 4th April 1959, No.31107 was presumably still allocated there, so it appears to have spent much of its long career in the area. It was withdrawn shortly after this picture was taken, being noted at Ashford Works four months later awaiting scrapping. The other locomotive in this illustration, 'Merchant Navy' Pacific No.35015 *Rotterdam Lloyd*, needs little introduction because, as mentioned elsewhere in this album, it was the sole rebuilt member of its class to work on the Eastern Section. *R. C. Riley*

An unidentified down train runs through Folkestone Warren behind bunker-first BR Standard Class 4MT 2-6-4T No.80065 on 29th May 1961. In 1888 a halt was opened in The Warren to bring visitors who wished to enjoy the distinctive landscape and ecology of this area. This was obviously a popular innovation because a tea room was constructed prior to the First World War to provide sustenance for the visitors. The halt closed just after the start of the Second World War. This spectacular section of line is probably better known for the notoriously unstable nature of the ground over which it runs, not to mention its extremely high maintenance costs. The chalk rests on a layer of gault clay which retards the percolation of rainwater, thus the weight of it increases considerably after heavy rain, causing the chalk to fall and create an undercliff alongside the tracks. Various measures have been tried to combat the problem, starting in 1948 when the land near the former halt was extended into the sea, the outer walls of this promontory being formed of $2\frac{1}{4}$ ton concrete blocks which were joined together with rails. Rock from Meldon Quarry was used as a base layer onto which 43,000 tons of chalk was deposited. This work is known as 'toe weighting'. When serious landslips occur this is bad enough but, unfortunately, two of the worst incidents during the last century occurred during wartime. On 19th December 1915 a major slip took place, closing the route until August 1919 and causing massive dislocation to both military and civilian traffic. A second wartime slip closed the line totally for six weeks from November 1939 until January 1940. *David Clark*

Another view of Folkestone Warren, taken on the same day as the previous picture, but this time looking eastwards with Abbot's Cliff forming the backdrop. Clouds of steam, in the distance above the wagons, indicate the position of the entrance to Abbotscliff tunnel (1 mile 182 yards). The short train of four Bulleid-designed coaches, hauled by Maunsell 'Schools' Class 4-4-0 No.30934 *St Lawrence*, appears to be a local working. The tiny Abbotscliff signal box, on the left, was merely a block post which controlled entry to a siding. The isolated section of line between Abbotscliff and Shakespeare tunnels has been the scene of some noteworthy events. In 1881 the SER obtained parliamentary approval for the construction of a Channel Tunnel and commenced boring near the western entrance to Shakespeare tunnel. The work was later halted, but not before coal deposits had been discovered which led to the establishment of the Kent coalfield. In the 1970s British Government approval was once again forthcoming and work recommenced, only to be cancelled by a later administration. On 20th January 1986 permission was again given and Eurotunnel moved onto the same site as previous attempts. *David Clark*

An unidentified rebuilt Bulleid Pacific negotiates the tight curve from Archcliffe Junction at the approach to Dover Marine station with the down 'Golden Arrow' on 12th May 1961, a month before regular steam workings bowed out on this route. The equally tightly curved tracks on the right led to Hawkesbury Street Junction and Dover Priory station. Dover Marine station (later renamed Western Docks) was built by the SECR immediately prior to the start of the First World War and was constructed on reclaimed land to the east of the Admiralty Pier. It opened for military traffic, principally ambulance trains, from 2nd January 1915, public passenger services commencing from 18th January 1919. It was a fine station, with an impressive stone frontage and two long island platforms situated beneath a high overall roof, and must have created a favourable 'first impression' on foreign visitors. The building in the background has appeared in countless views of this area over the years. It is the Lord Warden Hotel, constructed in 1851, and one of its dubious claims to fame is that Lt.Col. H. F. Stephens, well known for his involvement in many light railways up and down the country, was a long-term resident until his death in 1931.
John Langford

The up 'Golden Arrow', hauled by Bulleid Light Pacific No.34085 *501 Squadron*, creates a stirring and magnificent sight as it eases around the curve from Dover Marine station in June 1959. On the right a couple of engines, including SECR H Class 0-4-4T No.31542 nearest to the camera, can be seen simmering on Dover shed. The shed was originally located at Dover Priory, but in 1928 the SR constructed a new depot west of the newly opened Dover Marine station. It was positioned between the sea shore and the main line. Life at a steam shed was always hard, but in addition to the dirty and laborious work, the shed's exposed position afforded staff little protection from the elements. One can only imagine the nightmare of trying to empty ash from a locomotive's smokebox as it was being blown around by gale force winds coming in off the English Channel. Following the opening of the Channel Tunnel, most railway installations at Dover were rendered superfluous and have now been largely abandoned.
G. H. Hunt/Colour-Rail

Notices at the ends of station platforms are common enough, but there cannot be many locations where separate signs in three different languages were provided. This fine display of warning notices – the middle one is in French and the bottom sign in German – was photographed at Dover Priory station in 1959. Incredible though it may seem to some Britons, in a few European countries the railway tracks are actually a public right of way, although this presumably excludes stretches with a third (electrified) rail running through a tunnel, as seen here! These signs were doubtless photographed just after they had been erected – electric trains did not commence regular operation at Dover until mid-1959. *Michael Allen*

21

A portrait of Deal station on 23rd May 1959 showing Maunsell N Class 2-6-0 No.31852 rolling in with a local train to Dover. The train is composed of set No.190, four coaches also of Maunsell design, plus a van on the rear. The first railway to serve Deal was the SER's branch from Minster, opened on 1st July 1847. This line traversed flat terrain and was cheaply built. In complete contrast, the route from Dover crosses the Kentish Downs, which separate Dover from Deal, and is characterised by extremely heavy gradients and considerable earthworks. After passing Buckland Junction, where the former LCDR line to Faversham diverges, the line from Dover climbs tortuously for almost 2½ miles around a horseshoe curve, the gradient being as steep as 1 in 60 at one point, as it gains height running along the side of a valley. There are quite spectacular views looking across Dover to the English Channel and a summit is reached just after Guston tunnel. The first proposal for a line connecting Dover with Deal was made in 1862, but perhaps the promoters were put off by the difficult nature of the route and nothing happened. In 1874 the Dover & Deal Joint Railway was proposed, the first sod being cut on 29th June 1878 by the Lord Warden of the Cinque Ports, Earl Granville. This interesting, but rather obscure route, which made an end-on connection with the line from Minster, eventually opened to traffic on 15th June 1881. *John Edgington/Colour-Rail*

DOVER TO RAMSGATE

The headboard of the Railway Enthusiasts Club is positioned on the top lamp bracket of SECR O1 Class 0-6-0 No.31258 at Minster on 23rd May 1959. The locomotive was working a railtour of lines in the area which during the course of the day visited Deal and Tilmanstone colliery. James Stirling, Chief Mechanical Engineer of the SER, designed the O Class 0-6-0s for heavier goods services and a total of 122 were built at Ashford Works and by Sharp Stewart & Co. Construction lasted over a long period, the first examples appeared in 1878 and the final engine was produced in 1899. Commencing in 1903 Wainwright started reboilering the locomotives with a domed boiler and 58 had been rebuilt to O1 Class by 1927. More than 50 O1s came into BR ownership, but by the end of the 1950s only eight remained, primarily for use on lines with a light axle loading. All had gone by 1961, apart from one preserved example. *John Edgington*

ASHFORD TO RAMSGATE

The secondary line from Ashford to Ramsgate via Minster is arguably one of the most attractive in Kent. Double track throughout, it threads the pleasant Stour Valley and serves the delightful village of Chilham, in addition to the ancient cathedral city of Canterbury. The route was authorised in 1844 and opened throughout to Ramsgate Town by the SER on 13th April 1846. Originally, some trains continued from Ramsgate to Margate Sands station, but this link succumbed to closure when the Southern Railway reorganised operations in the Thanet area in 1926. Apart from its scenic attractions, the line is also well-known for its numerous manned and occupation level crossings. When the east Kent coalfield was still flourishing there was an unadvertised weekday service from Margate to Canterbury West which ran thrice daily to convey miners to Chislet Colliery Halt, which was about five miles north-east of Canterbury. Unfortunately, the route was rarely photographed in colour in steam days, so the author was pleased to locate this picture of H Class No.31324 pausing at Canterbury West with the 11.10am Margate to Ashford train on 4th February 1961. This was the only shot taken between Minster and Ashford submitted for inclusion in this album. Note the four-wheeled van on the rear of the passenger train in the adjacent platform. *John Langford*

Photographed on a sunny 28th March 1959, BR Standard Class 2MT 2-6-2T No.84021 makes a spirited exit from Ramsgate with an Ashford train. Note the depot in the background, where building work was apparently being undertaken in connection with the introduction of electric stock. Part of the old steam shed, which had been built in the mid-1920s, was incorporated in the emu inspection shed. No.84021 was one of ten of these locomotives allocated to Ashford shed for a brief period about this time. It was soon displaced by electrification, however, and in the early 1960s was based at Crewe Works for shunting purposes, together with a number of sister locomotives. It was condemned in August 1964 after a tragically brief working life and cut-up at Crewe later that year. *R. C. Riley*

THE CATFORD LOOP LINE

A spectacular pall of black smoke erupts from the chimney of unrebuilt 'Merchant Navy' Class Pacific No.35001 *Channel Packet* as it passes Ravensbourne, on the Catford Loop line, in charge of a down continental express some time in the late 1950s. The precise date of this photograph is unknown, but No.35001 was rebuilt in August 1959, so the picture must have been taken prior to this time. The Catford Loop was incorporated on 12th August 1889 by the nominally independent Shortlands & Nunhead Railway Company and opened on 1st July 1892. It has always been regarded as a relief to the main line, which could not be widened because of Penge tunnel. The Catford Loop line was among the first of the Eastern Section's suburban lines to be electrified, public services commencing from 12th July 1925. *Ken Wightman*

Gas lighting, ancient lower-quadrant semaphore signalling and the signal box (just visible above the roof of the train) all make it hard to believe that this picture was taken at Beckenham Junction station, in the late 1950s. The train is, of course, the unmistakable 'Golden Arrow' hauled by beautifully prepared BR Standard 'Britannia' Pacific No.70004 *William Shakespeare*. This locomotive, together with sister engine No.70014 *Iron Duke*, was transferred to the London Midland Region in May 1958, so this picture was taken prior to this date. It was reported at the time that the Southern Region exchanged their two 'Britannias' for a couple of BR Standard Class 5MT locomotives, Nos.73041 and 73042. One wonders which region obtained the better deal! *Ken Wightman*

BECKENHAM JUNCTION
TO FAVERSHAM

The eastbound 'Kentish Belle' from Victoria to Ramsgate, running on this occasion without its distinctive locomotive headboard, passes Bromley South behind BR Standard Class 5MT No.73080 in about 1958. This train started life as the 'Thanet Belle' in May 1948, following BR's decision to re-introduce all-Pullman services to the Kent coast resorts. In the summer 1951 timetable the train was revised as part of the Festival of Britain celebrations and a three-coach portion was detached at Faversham to serve Canterbury East, returning in the evening. The rest of the train continued to run to Ramsgate, serving most stations *en route*. It was decided that the train's title was no longer appropriate, and the name 'Kentish Belle' was adopted. In 1952, after the end of the Festival of Britain, the train reverted to the original arrangements, leaving Victoria at 11.35am on Mondays to Fridays and returning from Ramsgate at 5.05pm; different timings applied at the weekends. The name 'Kentish Belle' was retained. During the week motive power was normally a Bulleid Light Pacific, but at weekends, when locomotive resources were stretched to the limit, almost any available engine was rostered for the train, including 'Schools' and L Class 4-4-0s. The electrification of the Victoria to Ramsgate services from June 1959 heralded the introduction of a pattern of regular interval train services and the 'Kentish Belle' clearly did not fit in with the Southern Region's plans. The train ran for the last time on 14th September 1958, after a relatively brief career. *Ken Wightman*

An unidentified Maunsell U1 Class 2-6-0 leaves Bromley South on a sunny morning in the late 1950s hauling an express bound for Ramsgate. The train is made up of a rake of Maunsell coaches in carmine and cream livery. Another train, headed by D1 Class 4-4-0 No.31749, stands on an adjacent line, the crew looking on as the Ramsgate working accelerates away from the station. The train on the right appears to be standing in a siding, possibly waiting to reverse into the station to form a later train to the Kent Coast. Note the goods yard is still open for business and semaphore signalling is visible in the distance. *Ken Wightman*

Prior to the growth of private car ownership and development of the motorway network, most people desiring a day out by the seaside had little choice but to take the train. Special day excursion trains were run – usually with bargain fares to attract the masses – from inland towns to the Kent Coast resorts and here one of these workings is seen passing Bromley South, its destination apparently being Margate. The train is hauled by clean Stanier 'Black Five' No.45067 and largely formed of LMSR rolling stock, which suggests that the special originated somewhere on the London Midland Region! The exact date of the shot is unknown, but the picture is likely to have been taken on a Sunday because the Southern Region operating authorities are unlikely to have wanted this train on a Saturday, when their tracks would have been extremely congested. At least the sun was shining when the excursioners passed Bromley, which augered well for a good day on the beach! *Ken Wightman*

In the early 1950s two BR Standard 'Britannia' Pacifics – Nos.70004 *William Shakespeare* and 70014 *Iron Duke* – were allocated to Stewarts Lane shed primarily for use on the famous 'Golden Arrow' express boat train between London and Dover. During this period Stewarts Lane shed had a richly deserved reputation for turning out locomotives in sparkling condition, so the sight of a gleaming 'Britannia' Pacific at the head of an equally immaculate set of Pullman carriages must have been a tonic for ordinary citizens in the drab years following World War II. The Pacifics were not confined to the 'Arrow', however, and in this shot No.70014 *Iron Duke* is seen approaching Shortlands at the head of another down continental express, sometime in the late 1950s. On this occasion *Iron Duke* is not in its usual exemplary condition, so perhaps its sister locomotive was the regular 'Arrow' engine at that time. In 1958 the two 'Britannias' were re-allocated to Trafford Park shed (Manchester) and were used on London expresses via the Peak route. Needless to say there was a marked decline in their external condition, their glory days on the 'Golden Arrow' being well and truly over. This is one of many memorable photographs in this album taken by the late Ken Wightman who, at one time, occupied a house adjacent to the railway line at this location.

In this view 'Merchant Navy' Class Pacific No.35015 *Rotterdam Lloyd* is seen heading a down continental express between Beckenham Junction and Shortlands. In the late 1950s No.35015 was one of a trio of these locomotives – the others were Nos.35001 *Channel Packet* and 35028 *Clan Line* – based at Stewarts Lane shed for use on the heaviest Eastern Section passenger workings. At that time members of the 'Merchant Navy' Class were being rebuilt at Eastleigh Works and the Southern Region apparently preferred to concentrate the rebuilt examples on the Western Section, where the Bournemouth, Weymouth and West of England services were much more demanding than any of the duties undertaken by Stewarts Lane's engines. In fact, it must be admitted, the Eastern Section locomotives led a very quiet life compared to their Western Section counterparts. *Rotterdam Lloyd* was rebuilt at Eastleigh in June 1958 and, most surprisingly, returned to Stewarts Lane, becoming the only rebuilt member of its class to work regularly on the Eastern section. When Phase One of the Kent Coast Electrification Scheme was inaugurated in June 1959 all three members of the class were transferred to Nine Elms shed and Nos.35001 and 35028 were consequently among the last to be rebuilt. In February 1964 No.35015 became an early withdrawal casualty following a decision to cease general repairs on the 'Merchant Navy' Class and was scrapped by the romantically-named Slag Reduction Company of Rotherham. *Ken Wightman*

An excursion to Sheerness passes Downsbridge Road overbridge, between Beckenham Junction and Shortlands, behind Q Class No.30534, sometime in the late 1950s. Richard Maunsell's Q Class 0-6-0s were introduced in 1938 for secondary goods and passenger duties, but by the standards of that time were not particularly large or powerful. Initially, the Q class was only used on modest duties such as pick-up goods trains or short passenger workings, but shedmasters could not resist the temptation to employ their new acquisitions on more demanding main-line duties for which they were not suited. Complaints by footplatemen about the inadequate performance of the class started at about the same time! In the late 1940s modifications were carried out which improved the class's performance, but even so the use of No.30534 on the train seen here is unlikely to have had the wholehearted approval of the enginemen. Apart from visits to Ashford Works for repair, the Qs were uncommon on the Eastern Section. During its career No.30534 saw service at Eastleigh, Redhill, Tunbridge Wells West and Norwood Junction, and was one of the first of its class to be withdrawn, an event which occurred in December 1962. *Ken Wightman*

In this wintry scene Maunsell 'King Arthur' Class 4-6-0 No.30767 *Sir Valence* is depicted heading a Victoria to Ramsgate train near Shortlands Junction, probably in early 1959. No.30767 was built by the North British Locomotive Company, Glasgow, in June 1925 and remained in service until June 1959. The uniform rake of coaches forming the train appears to be Set No.474, an 8-car set of Bulleid stock which was allocated to the London to Ramsgate services. Six of the vehicles, including the two brake coaches, were second class only, while two coaches were composites, which offered both first and second class accommodation. The set had a total of 48 first and 392 second class seats. *Ken Wightman*

A rather grimy 'King Arthur' class 4-6-0, which appears to be No.30776 *Sir Galagars*, is depicted heading for Victoria near Shortlands with an up continental express in the late 1950s. The train is formed of a remarkable variety of coaches ranging from late-1920s Maunsell stock, post World War II Bulleid vehicles and the (then) relatively modern BR Standard coaches. *Ken Wightman*

In pre-war times double-heading of the 'Night Ferry' by a couple of SECR 4-4-0s was customary, but when the train was re-introduced in 1947 a single Bulleid Pacific sufficed, assisted by a 4-4-0 when its weight limit was exceeded. In October 1949 three 'Merchant Navy' Class locomotives were transferred to Dover to work the service unassisted, their duty comprising the up 'Night Ferry' and a boat train working from and to Victoria before returning to Dover with the evening 'Night Ferry'. During steam days the locomotive duty had generally been the preserve of Dover shed and enginemen. Towards the end of regular steam working Bulleid's 'Battle of Britain' Class engines, based at Stewarts Lane shed, were more regularly seen. Over the years quite a selection of motive power worked the 'Night Ferry' at various times, including BR Standard 'Britannia' Pacifics for a brief period in 1952/53. During the following year trials were conducted with the SR's main-line diesel-electric locomotives, while at odd times Dover shed provided a 'Schools' Class 4-4-0 to assist the up train, which was booked to travel via the Chatham line from September 1954. The last recorded occasion when the 'Night Ferry' was steam-worked was New Year's Day 1962 when an N Class 2-6-0 assisted 'West Country' Pacific No.34100 *Appledore* on the up train. The 'Night Ferry' will best be remembered, however, for the interesting combination of a Bulleid Pacific piloted by a SECR 4-4-0, and in this shot D1 Class No.31743 is seen assisting 'Battle of Britain' Class No.34073 *249 Squadron* near Shortlands on the up service. The proposal to run a through London to Paris train using a ferry was first considered by the board of the Southern Railway in 1930, but there were various wrangles with the French who initially wanted a Calais to Richborough service. It was at about this time that the SR first intimated that it proposed to run an overnight passenger service. Eventually it was agreed that the service would operate between Dover and Dunkerque, and in early 1933 three new coal-fired train ferries were ordered. Approval was also given for construction of a special loading dock at Dover and twelve new Wagon-Lits sleeping cars were specially designed for the train. The inauguration ceremony for the new service took place on 12th October 1936, and the first public working left London at 10pm on 14th October. Unfortunately, bad weather in the English Channel often caused delays, and there were reports of the sleeping cars shuttling to and fro on board the ships. These factors proved to be the Achilles' heel of the 'Night Ferry' operation throughout its life. Services were suspended during the war, but resumed in December 1947. Departure time from London was usually 10pm, arrival in Paris being made around 9am the following morning. In 1957 through sleeping cars to Brussels were conveyed for the first time, and in the early 1960s the train reached the height of its popularity. From 2nd December 1963 the loading was increased to nineteen vehicles, including ten sleeping cars, three buffet or restaurant cars, three ordinary coaches for 'walking' passengers and three vans. This mammoth load of 851½ tons was the heaviest regular passenger train on British Railways. At the end of 1967 Basle became another destination served by the train, although this was purely a seasonal venture provided for winter sports enthusiasts. Towards the end of the 1960s the growth of air travel was starting to have a marked effect on the 'Night Ferry's passenger carryings, as diplomats and businessmen found that the airlines offered increasingly reliable and much more convenient services. BR decided that from June 1975 foot passengers would be conveyed in emu stock, this strange decision further undermining the economics of running the 'Night Ferry'. In the spring of 1980 it came as no surprise when it was announced that the train would be discontinued from the end of October. Patronage had been reduced to a derisory 37 passengers on average each way nightly and, crucially, the cost of the long overdue replacement sleeping cars could not be justified. The train ran for the last time on 31st October 1980 behind a Class 33 diesel, which sported a replica old-style headboard specially made by the staff at Stewarts Lane. By sheer coincidence this was also the last day of publication of the 'London Evening News', which was reportedly read by the driver prior to departure. Thus after more than thirty years of operation BR rid itself of this unique train, no doubt to concentrate on the much more important matter of providing extra services for Tunbridge Wells commuters! *Ken Wightman*

It was certainly not unknown for double-headed Bulleid Pacifics to be seen at the head of the 'Night Ferry' but, as far as the author is aware, this remarkable sight was rarely photographed in colour. The train was actually booked to be hauled by two Bulleids for a time during late 1956. Unfortunately the date of this picture, taken near Shortlands, is not known. *Ken Wightman*

Bulleid 'Merchant Navy' Class Pacific No.35001 *Channel Packet* emits a volcanic smoke effect as it approaches Shortlands Junction with the 9am Victoria to Folkestone Harbour boat train on a glorious morning in the late 1950s. The train appears to be accelerating away from a signal check or permanent way slowing just as the fireman was at work – hence the clouds of black smoke. Note the remarkable selection of coaches which form the first part of the train. The leading vehicle is of Maunsell design, while the second coach is a Bulleid-designed carriage in carmine and cream colours. The third coach is, of course, a Pullman car in its unmistakable traditional Pullman livery. In the 1958 summer timetable the 9am boat train from Victoria connected with the 11.20am boat from Folkestone to Boulogne, giving an arrival time in the Gare du Nord, Paris, at 5.06pm. *Ken Wightman*

Pictured from the old Shortlands Junction signal box, Maunsell 'King Arthur' Class 4-6-0 No.30793 *Sir Ontzlake* is seen taking the down fast line with a Victoria to Ramsgate express. No.30793 was built at Eastleigh Works in March 1926 and survived to become one of the final members of its class, lasting until August 1962. The junction of the Victoria to Bromley South and Catford Loop lines (seen on the right) at Shortlands was remodelled as part of a major programme to modernise the permanent way prior to the electrification of Kent Coast services. The work, which was undertaken in various stages between May and October 1958, involved realignment of many tight curves and, crucially, the rearrangement of the running lines. The track layout between Shortlands and Bickley Junctions formerly consisted of four electrified tracks with parallel working of two down lines and two up lines. This caused conflicting movements, and the proposals for modernisation consisted of pairing the up and down fast, plus the up and down slow lines in order to minimise the number of locations where the paths of trains cut across each other. Note the new Shortlands Junction signal box which is partially visible. *Ken Wightman*

In this June 1960 photograph, Bulleid 'Battle of Britain' Pacific No.34067 *Tangmere* is depicted passing Valley Road pumping station, near Shortlands, with the 10.45am Victoria to Dover Marine boat train. The platform awnings just visible in the far distance are those of Shortlands station. *Tangmere* was a product of Brighton Works, being outshopped in September 1947, and the locomotive lasted in BR service until withdrawn in November 1963. Fortunately, No.34067 was one of a large number of Bulleid Pacifics sold to Messrs. Woodham Bros. of Barry, South Wales, and it rested in their scrap yard until purchased for preservation. At the time of writing it is nearing the end of a lengthy restoration and is expected to return to traffic in the near future. *Paul Leavens*

This picture shows Maunsell Class U1 2-6-0 No.31907 approaching St Mary Cray Junction with a London-bound train on 18th May 1959. The headcode indicates a Dover to Victoria via Chatham working. These locomotives were a three cylinder development of the same designer's U Class engines, but they only numbered 21 examples. The device on the right is a Civil Engineer's Dept. tamping machine. *R. C. Riley*

A down freight train from Hither Green sidings passes St Mary Cray Junction behind Maunsell N Class 'Mogul' No.31871, which is in rather neglected external condition. Judging by the incomplete alterations to the track layout, this picture was probably taken in early 1959. Some of the most extensive track alterations carried out in connection with the Kent Coast electrification were undertaken in this area. The scheme involved quadrupling the five miles-long section from Bickley Junction to Swanley Junction, where the lines to Chatham and Maidstone diverge. The quadrupling necessitated the rebuilding of eleven overbridges in addition to the construction of a new viaduct at St Mary Cray. *Ken Wightman*

One of the most demanding sections on the Victoria to Ramsgate line is Sole Street bank, which involves five miles of 1 in 100 gradient against westbound trains. It was unfortunate that enginemen of London-bound trains were faced with this obstacle towards the end of the journey, but at least they did not have to contend with a 'cold' engine! In this illustration Maunsell N Class 2-6-0 No.31411 is seen hard at work with a Ramsgate to Victoria service in August 1958. The three coaches immediately behind the locomotive formed a set of three BR Standard vehicles. No.31411 survived to become one of the last engines of its class in traffic and in the mid-1960s was regularly employed on enthusiasts' specials on the Central and South Western Divisions. Almost needless to say it was maintained in pristine condition for these duties in marked contrast to its filthy state in this picture. *Ken Wightman*

Once past St Mary Cray, eastbound trains leave behind London's continuous suburban sprawl. This shot depicts an evening Cannon Street to Ramsgate express descending Sole Street bank, between Swanley and Rochester, with Bulleid 'West Country' Pacific No.34012 *Launceston* in charge. Note that the rolling stock, also of Bulleid design, is in carmine and cream livery. The line from St Mary Cray to Strood was originally proposed by the East Kent Railway, the necessary powers being obtained in 1858. The line opened on 3rd December 1860, by which time the East Kent Company had changed its name to the London, Chatham & Dover Railway (LCDR), although the company's route from Canterbury to Dover did not open until July 1861. The St Mary Cray to Strood section was cheaply built, and has fierce gradients in both directions and some tight curves. The line crosses the North Downs, against the grain of deep and steep-sided valleys, the latter being crossed at St Mary Cray and Farningham Road by high viaducts. *Ken Wightman*

A general view of the shed yard at Gillingham, with C Class 0-6-0 No.31692 on the left and H Class 0-4-4T No.31548 on the right. Note the façade of the shed building, which was still impressive despite the ugly floodlights and liberal coating of soot. Gillingham shed – which mainly provided locomotives for local freight duties – did not include any of the more illustrious steam locomotive classes on its allocation and probably attracted few photographers, so this shot is likely to be something of a rarity. The picture was taken in June 1959, just before the shed's closure as an independent depot with the introduction of electric working to Ramsgate. It remained open to service visiting locomotives for some time afterwards. Both of these engines were designed by Harry S. Wainwright for the South Eastern & Chatham Railway. No.31548 was built at Ashford Works in December 1904. It was a Gillingham resident at the time of this picture, was made redundant by electrification and moved to Brighton, but failed to find favour there and was withdrawn two months later. No.31692 was constructed by Neilson, Reid & Co. of Glasgow in July 1900 and was apparently a visitor from Hither Green shed when this shot was taken. It lasted in traffic until April 1960. *G. H. Hunt/Colour-Rail*

In this vintage shot a beautifully turned-out SECR D Class 4-4-0, No.31737, is seen pausing at Rainham with a special working in September 1954. In the author's opinion the D Class is one of the classic British designs, an outstandingly attractive and graceful machine. The first examples of this class – nicknamed 'Coppertops' by the enginemen – entered traffic in 1901 and a total of 51 engines was eventually built by Ashford Works and a variety of private firms, notably Dubs & Co and Sharp Stewart & Co. The class was initially put to work on the lines from London to Dover and Hastings, but they could later be seen throughout Kent working the heaviest express services until the introduction of the larger L Class 4-4-0s, which took over the most demanding duties. Following the rebuilding of many of the D class by Maunsell in the 1920s, the Ds in original condition drifted onto less exacting tasks but could still be observed on relief continental boat trains up to the start of the Second World War. The excellence of this class was officially recognised in the late 1950s when No.31737 was earmarked for preservation as part of the National Collection and subsequently spent a period in store at Tweedmouth shed, Northumberland, before returning to its old haunts at Ashford for restoration in late 1959. The locomotive is now part of the National Collection at York.
J. B. C. McCann/Colour-Rail

Photographed on 13th June 1959, the penultimate day of regular main line steam operation in the area, SECR D1 Class 4-4-0 No.31749 makes a smoky departure from Newington with the 11.50am Victoria to Dover Priory train. This working was fast from London to Chatham, but beyond there became an 'all stations' train and was scheduled to arrive at Dover at 2.45pm. A 2¼ miles-long section of line between Rainham and Newington was quadrupled as part of Phase One of the Kent Coast Electrification Scheme, thus enabling fast trains to overtake stopping services. The work involved excavating 94,000 cubic yards of material from the cuttings, the spoil being used to widen the embankments on other parts of the line. In addition, eight bridges were reconstructed or widened and the station at Newington was partially rebuilt with a footbridge and new platforms. *R. C. Riley*

FAVERSHAM TO RAMSGATE

Despite the dark and menacing clouds, the sun was shining on SECR L class 4-4-0 No.31781 as it left Faversham with a Dover-bound train on 30th September 1958, proving that occasionally railway photographers have good fortune on their side! The route from Faversham to Ramsgate was proposed by independent companies and opened in stages, the first section, as far as Whitstable, carrying its first passengers on 1st August 1860. The route was opened to Herne Bay on 13th July 1861 while the final section to Ramsgate was commissioned on 5th October 1863. Services along this line were provided by the LCDR from the outset. Note the shiny new third-rail insulation pots which had been laid preparatory to electrification in June 1959. The long footbridge, on the right, gave generations of train spotters an excellent vantage point from where to observe operations at this busy junction, and also a bird's eye view of the locomotive shed which is partially visible. *R. C. Riley*

After almost one hundred years of steam traction, services along the north Kent Coast line were revolutionised from 15th June 1959 when Phase One of BR's Kent Coast Electrification Scheme came into operation. In this portrait, Maunsell 'Schools' 4-4-0 No.30921 *Shrewsbury* is seen steaming along between Chestfield & Swalecliffe Halt and Herne Bay with an unidentified down train on 14th June – the very last day of regular steam working. The photographer recalls that he returned to London that evening on the last up Chatham line steam train, the 8.56pm Ramsgate to Blackheath, which was in charge of a SECR 4-4-0 hauling 9-set No.917 – a tough proposition for one of these moderately powered engines. The locomotive was in the capable hands of a Hither Green crew who were assisted for part of the run by two enthusiasts – an 'unofficial' driver and fireman! Despite the apparently crowded footplate, Blackheath was reached four minutes before time. *John Langford*

Another picture taken during the dying days of steam on the Chatham line, this time showing an unidentified Victoria to Ramsgate train near Herne Bay in June 1959. Motive power is provided by Maunsell U1 Class 2-6-0 No.31904. This class, which first saw the light of day in 1928, was a development of the same designer's U Class 2-6-0s. The U1s had three cylinders and were marginally more powerful. The line between Herne Bay and Birchington is perhaps best known for the catastrophic flooding which occurred in February 1953, causing severe damage to the track between those points. This stretch was closed for several months and Herne Bay became the terminus of a shuttle service from Faversham. Some trains from the Kent coast to London started from Birchington, from where they went to Ramsgate where engines were changed. From Ramsgate they would have taken the line to Canterbury West, and continued to Faversham using a temporary connection between the SER and LCDR routes at Canterbury. Hundreds of trains of chalk were run to rebuild the formation near Reculver followed by 60 trainloads of ballast from Meldon Quarry. Services were eventually restored on 21st May 1953. *G. H. Hunt/Colour-Rail*

On a bright 28th March 1959, BR Standard Class 5MT 4-6-0 No.73083 (later named *Pendragon*) runs into Margate station with an up express. The first route to serve Margate was a 34 miles-long branch from Ashford via Ramsgate (Town), opened by the SER to Margate (Sands) station on 1st December 1846. This provided a most unsatisfactory and extremely circuitous journey from Margate to London. When the LCDR route from Faversham was put forward in the early 1860s, a terminal station at Margate was envisaged and suitable land was purchased. An extension to Ramsgate was, however, approved soon afterwards and the plans quickly altered to incorporate a through station, named Margate West. The ground acquired for the terminal station was used for goods and locomotive sheds instead. One of the first acts of the newly-formed Southern Railway was to rationalise the routes in the Margate/Ramsgate area. Incredibly, as a result of rivalry between the SER and LCDR both towns had two main stations, so the SR proposed a new link line in the area which had the effect of unifying the two hitherto largely separate systems. This new line was brought into use from 2nd July 1926, from which date Margate Sands station was closed and Margate West (which lost its suffix) subsequently became the only station in the town. *R. C. Riley*

In an everyday scene that will probably be familiar to many readers, passengers wait on the platform as the 4.40pm Ramsgate to Victoria train rounds the curve at the approach to Margate station with 'Schools' Class 4-4-0 No.30912 *Downside* in charge. But, actually, this shot is not quite so 'everyday' as it appears, because it was taken on the final day of steam operation, 14th June 1959, so this is another 'last day' picture of considerable historical significance. From the following morning trains would be formed of electric units, providing a faster, more frequent and hopefully, punctual service. But would they have that indefinable magic and irresistible appeal of a steam locomotive? Not likely! *Colour-Rail*

Another photograph taken on the last day of timetabled steam operation on the London to Chatham/Ramsgate line. The location and locomotive depicted do not require extensive explanation! At the time of this picture the station seen here was only 33 years old, having been constructed (as previously mentioned) on a new section of line in the mid-1920s. The new station replaced the SER's Ramsgate Town and the LCDR's Ramsgate Harbour stations, both of which were cramped and operationally inconvenient. Trains travelling from London to Margate via Ashford were forced to reverse at Ramsgate Town, while Ramsgate Harbour station was at the end of a 1,630 yards-long tunnel through which trains descended at 1 in 75. The Harbour station dated from 5th October 1863 and was probably best known for its strange and unusual location, sandwiched between the cliffs under the East Cliff Promenade and the Esplanade. Enthusiastic holiday-makers arriving at the station could reach the beach in under a minute if they hurried! A new locomotive shed and carriage servicing depot were built adjacent to the new Ramsgate station, the station's only drawback being its remote position from the town centre and holiday beaches. *Colour-Rail*

Photographed in June 1959 shortly before the start of regular electric working, the 7.37am train from Faversham to Dover is illustrated leaving Canterbury East station. Motive power is provided by SECR L1 Class No.31788. Note that the conductor rails are in position and there is a rake of 2-HAP electric stock in the adjacent siding. The 48½ miles-long section from Strood to Canterbury was authorised on 4th August 1853, the line being opened as far as Faversham in early 1858 under the auspicies of the East Kent Railway, which later became the LCDR. The section onwards to Canterbury East languished due to shortage of funds, but was eventually opened on 9th July 1860. Dover was reached in July 1861, thus completing a through route to the port which rivalled the South Eastern Railway's line via Ashford. *G. H. Hunt/Colour-Rail*

FAVERSHAM TO DOVER

In another shot taken during the last few days of timetabled steam operation on the Faversham-Canterbury East-Dover section, 'Schools' Class 4-4-0 No.30909 *St Paul's* is depicted drawing into Shepherdswell station with the 4.15pm Faversham to Dover working in June 1959.
G. H. Hunt/Colour-Rail

THE TILMANSTONE COLLIERY BRANCH

Tilmanstone colliery's pithead winding gear, seen in the background of this photograph, may seem totally alien in a county known as the 'garden of England', but the fact remains that east Kent had a flourishing mining industry for more than 70 years. Geologists had long predicted that coal lay beneath the chalk of east Kent, and they were proved correct in 1890 when boreholes put down at Dover in connection with the Channel Tunnel located coal seams at a depth of 1,157feet. In the early years of the 20th century many mines were established, however flooding and unfavourable geological conditions caused most to fail, but four were successful. At their peak in the 1930s the four mines (the others were Betteshanger, Chislet and Snowdown) produced around two million tons of coal per annum, a tiny amount compared to other, much larger coalfields but, even so, the collieries made a substantial contribution to the prosperity of east Kent and brought considerable freight traffic to the railway. Tilmanstone was served from the start by the East Kent Light Railway, which was promoted in 1910 by Kent Coal Concessions Ltd. and engineered by Colonel H. F. Stephens, a notable pioneer of light railways. The line opened in 1912 and Tilmanstone mine became productive during the following year, most of its output being taken by rail to the main line junction at Shepherdswell, 2½ miles distant. The East Kent Light Railway was later extended in stages to Wingham and Sandwich, but it served a thinly populated area and was largely closed shortly after nationalisation in 1948. Tilmanstone colliery, however, continued to be served by (what had become) a short BR branch from Shepherdswell and substantial investment in the early 1950s resulted in increased production to half a million tons annually. The colliery ceased production during the coal strike of 1984/85 and was officially closed in October 1986. Tilmanstone colliery's rail connection was closed from the end of the following year. In this splendid mid-1950s picture, Stirling O1 Class 0-6-0 No.31258 is seen near Eythorne crossing hauling ten wagons of coal to Shepherdswell. At this time up to nine trains, each composed of ten wagons, were despatched each weekday. The reign of the O1 Class on this duty lasted until May 1960 when it was displaced by diesel shunters. *Colour-Rail*

THE BROMLEY NORTH BRANCH

The short 1½ mile long branch from Grove Park, on the main line from Charing Cross to Tonbridge, to Bromley North was proposed by the Bromley Direct Company and opened for business on 1st January 1878. On 21st July 1879 this independent company was absorbed by the SER. The old market town of Bromley was described in an 1876 guide as being 'easy of access and consequently much in favour with City merchants'. Much to the frustration of the SER, for many years the rival LCDR had the monopoly of the Bromley traffic, but this situation dramatically changed when the Bromley North branch opened. The branch was electrified from 28th February 1926, from which date electric services were also introduced to Orpington and on the Hayes and Addiscombe branches. It had been planned to start running electric trains from 1st December 1925, but this idea had to be abandoned because the necessary electric power could not be supplied by that date. By way of compensation, however, at least a brand new station came into use at Bromley North during that month, replacing the previous premises which were in an extremely dilapidated condition, reputedly one of the worst stations on the former SECR system. The new station consisted of handsome buildings with generous platform awnings. Following electrification the Bromley North branch lapsed into obscurity, becoming merely a rather anonymous part of the 'Southern Electric' network. The branch did, however, have its exciting moments, if that is an appropriate description, because on 29th October 1962 an empty, unattended electric unit ran away from the station and covered the whole line before crashing into a bridge abutment at the north end of Grove Park station. In this illustration, presumably taken in the late 1950s, a very grimy LBSCR C2X Class 0-6-0, No.32551, is depicted in the goods yard at Bromley North. The second 'dome' on the boiler originally housed a top feed arrangement, but this was later discarded, although the 'dome' was left on the boiler top. The outline of the station building, with its small cupola, is just visible behind the goods wagons. *Ken Wightman*

THE WESTERHAM BRANCH

The SER first obtained powers to construct a branch from Dunton Green to Westerham in the early 1860s, but failed to exercise them. Eventually local landowners and traders secured the incorporation of the independent Westerham Valley Railway in 1876. The original aim of the promoters was to project the line beyond Westerham to connect with the LBSCR at Oxted, but the SER refused to co-operate with the Westerham company unless this part of the scheme was abandoned. The local company was forced to yield on this point and, in June 1879, the SER agreed to manage, maintain and operate the branch. The line opened for business on 7th July 1881. The $4\frac{3}{4}$ miles-long route was built as a double track line, but only one line was laid. At first there was only one intermediate station, Brasted, but in 1907 the SER added Chevening Halt which was situated about $1\frac{1}{2}$ miles from the main line junction at Dunton Green. In 1955 services along the branch were reduced to rush hours only as a result of declining patronage and were henceforth operated on a 'one engine in steam' basis. An interesting facet of the signalling arrangements at Dunton Green was an endless wireway which was used for the exchange of the single line tablets between the engine crews and the signalman. This ran between the London end of the up platform and the signal cabin, which was situated on the other side of the main line. When the main line was electrified in 1934 this was considered to be a hazard if the wire broke and came into contact with the third rail, so this ingenious device was taken out of use. In this view, taken on 12th July 1959, H Class 0-4-4T locomotive No.31518 is seen awaiting departure from Dunton Green with the 3.50pm train to Westerham. The vintage coaches were originally constructed by the SECR in 1905/06 as rail motor carriages, the leading end of each vehicle being supported by a separate engine unit. They saw service on the Isle of Wight, but returned to the mainland in 1927. They were converted for orthodox operation on the Hundred of Hoo line and later moved to the Westerham branch. *Michael Allen*

No.31518 is seen again, this time near Chevening Halt on 28th October 1961, the final day of passenger services along the branch, hence the Union flag tied to the front of the engine. During the line's twilight years H Class locomotives were the staple motive power, but other types including J Class 0-6-4Ts, SER O1 0-6-0s and *ex*-LCDR R and R1 Class 0-4-4Ts also made brief appearances at various times. On 15th January 1957 Bulleid Light Pacific No.34017 *Illfracombe* worked an 11-coach special to Kensington Olympia. The train was too long for the loop at Westerham so another engine had to be provided at the other end of the train. *David Clark*

In this attractive shot, the early morning sun highlights the exhaust of H Class 0-4-4T No.31543 as it romps through the fields soon after leaving Chevening Halt with the 8.26am train from Dunton Green in March 1961. *Paul Leavens*

Another view of the branch terminus at Westerham showing quite smart looking H Class 0-4-4T No.31308 waiting to return to Dunton Green on 9th September 1961. By this time the ancient coaches seen in other pictures had been replaced by much more comfortable Maunsell vehicles, which were converted for push-pull working in the late 1950s. Westerham's 13-lever signal box, which is just visible, survived until the end. In the early days there was a requirement for a locomotive to stable overnight, for which a small engine shed was provided. The introduction of rail-motors in 1906 rendered the shed redundant, but it was not demolished until 1925.
Dennis Ovenden

H Class No.31517 'blows off' at Westerham prior to departure with a train to Dunton Green sometime in the late 1950s. This picture illustrates the reasonably spacious terminus and part of the goods shed on the left. Note the splendid hostelry which was no doubt an ideal refuge for weary travellers if the branch train service was dislocated for some reason. *Ken Wightman*

REDHILL TO TONBRIDGE

Opened in May 1842, the Redhill to Tonbridge line was originally part of the SER's main line from London to Dover until the Sevenoaks cut-off was brought into use in 1868. One of the construction engineer's reports stated that the stations had been constructed at 'moderate cost'. Perhaps 'minimum cost' would have been a more accurate description, because most had simple single-storey wooden clapboard buildings and staggered platforms with a foot crossing rather than a footbridge. One of the most interesting and unusual features of the line occurs where it passes over the Oxted to Uckfield route about a mile west of Edenbridge. The latter runs in Little Browns tunnel at this point, but is opened out where the former SER line crosses over it on a bridge. Here, a Redhill-bound train is seen in the early 1960s with BR Standard Class 4MT No.76053 in charge.
Paul Leavens

Despite the amount of cloud in the sky in this picture the photographer was lucky enough to have the sun shining brightly on the subject at the crucial moment! In this shot SECR L Class 4-4-0 No.31777 is depicted heading eastwards at Bough Beech, between Edenbridge and Penshurst, apparently with a local working in the late 1950s. No.31777 was one of ten machines ordered from A. Borsig of Tegel, Berlin, the remaining twelve being built by Beyer, Peacock & Co. of Manchester. The former firm gained the order due to the inability of a British manufacturer to guarantee delivery by August 1914. It is recorded that the first two engines arrived at Dover on 24th May 1914 in a partially dismantled state, and the whole batch had been delivered by 11th June. They were prepared for traffic at Ashford Works by the maker's fitters who also travelled on the footplate when trial runs took place on the main line. The 'foreign' locomotives were fitted with Schmidt-pattern superheaters, which were much easier on maintenance than the Robinson variety used on the British-built engines. No.31777 was probably nearing the end of its life when this picture was taken, being withdrawn in September 1959. *Ken Wightman*

Another illustration taken at Bough Beech, presumably on the same day as the previous shot. Once again, the photographer has been lucky with the sun! Here, another SECR L Class, No.31772, is depicted, this time heading westwards towards Redhill with a local passenger working. *Ken Wightman*

An up local train, headed by BR Standard Class 4MT 2-6-4T locomotive No.80043, leaves Penshurst some time in the early 1960s. Like so many wayside stations, Penshurst has lost most of its facilities over the years. The buildings on the up platform were gutted by fire in 1924 and replaced by a Tudor-style structure in the following year. This lasted until about the early 1970s. Goods facilities were withdrawn from 9th September 1963, while the signal box was taken out of use in March 1986 and demolished soon afterwards. No.80043 was one of many BR-built 2-6-4T locomotives active in the Redhill and Tonbridge areas in the early 1960s and hardly had a high profile. Later in its career, however, it was transferred to the legendary Somerset & Dorset line, and was one of two engines which powered the final public passenger working over the Templecombe to Bath section in March 1966. *Ken Wightman*

OXTED TO TUNBRIDGE WELLS WEST

The Oxted to Tunbridge Wells West line was constructed in stages, the principal section from Hurst Green Junction, just south of Oxted, to Ashurst Junction (near Groombridge) being opened on 1st October 1888. In this picture SECR H Class 0-4-4T No.31533, which is in pristine condition, propels an Oxted to Tunbridge Wells push-pull train near Hever on 14th May 1960. Push-pull services of this type were also known as motor trains. Trains on this line started their journey in Surrey, but soon crossed the county border into Kent. They then crossed and re-crossed the Kent/East Sussex border four times before reaching their destination. This line once formed part of a busy network of secondary lines which offered an alternative to the Brighton Line in emergencies. Sadly, the only remnant existing nowadays is the long branch line to Uckfield. The section from Eridge to Tunbridge Wells was closed in 1985, while the Uckfield to Lewes link was severed in 1969. *David Clark*

SECR H Class 0-4-4T No.31518 leaves Mark Beech tunnel with an Oxted to Tunbridge Wells West working in June 1963, and is about to call at Cowden station, which is a few hundred yards behind the photographer. About a mile south of the station the line crosses the county border, which is formed by Kent Water (river), into East Sussex. By the date of this picture most workings in this area were in the hands of 3-car 'Oxted' diesel multiple units. No.31518, which was built at Ashford Works in July 1909, was one of the last three members of its class in traffic, lasting until early 1964. *Roy Hobbs*

Pictured on a lovely summer's evening, Maunsell Q Class 0-6-0 No.30549 pulls away from Ashurst with the
4.49pm Victoria to Tunbridge Wells West train. This picture was taken in June 1962. The locomotive is sporting
a rather ugly stovepipe chimney which was fitted at Swindon Works in 1955 when the engine was undergoing
draughting and steaming trials. Despite being the final member of its class to be built, in September 1939,
No.30549 was among the first to be condemned, in July 1963. Like most stations on this picturesque, but thinly
populated stretch of line, Ashurst station only serves a small village. Once again, the county border with East
Sussex is not far away – in this case the boundary is formed by the river Medway, which is just behind the
photographer. *J. Spencer Gilks*

Looking at this May 1963 view of Tunbridge Wells West station, with its impressive signal gantry and bustling engine shed, it is sad to reflect that the station is no longer part of the national rail system. Until the mid-1960s it was still the hub of a network of services which fanned out to Eastbourne, Brighton, Three Bridges and Redhill via Tonbridge. In addition there were trains to Oxted and London termini. At one time the line from Groombridge, where four of these routes converged, to Tunbridge Wells carried up to four trains an hour in each direction. Unfortunately, most of these predominantly rural and lightly-used lines were recommended for closure in the Beeching Plan for 'reshaping' the railway system, the first casualty being the delightful 'Cuckoo' line to Eastbourne, which lost its passenger trains in 1965. The services to Three Bridges and Oxted quickly followed and trains no longer ran through to Brighton after the Uckfield to Lewes route was shut in 1969. After this, Tunbridge Wells West station continued to be served by an Eridge to Tonbridge shuttle service, but it must have been hopelessly uneconomic and this ran for the last time in 1985, when the station closed. The 'reshaping' of Tunbridge Wells West had been completed! Despite this retrenchment, some of the infrastructure seen here still remains *in situ*, most notably the locomotive shed, now used by a preservation group which operates as far as Groombridge. The fine station building, with its magnificent tower, part of which is just visible in the middle of the picture, has listed building status and found a new lease of life as a restaurant after the closure of the railway. *Ken Wightman*

TONBRIDGE TO TUNBRIDGE WELLS WEST

SECR C Class 0-6-0 No.31716, in rather neglected external condition, attacks the 1 in 53 to 1 in 47 climb away from Tonbridge with a train to Brighton on 4th June 1961. This section of line was heavily graded against southbound trains as they climbed towards the Sussex Weald. No.31716 was a Sharp Stewart product of 1900 vintage, and at this time was one of a handful of these engines based at Tonbridge shed for local passenger and freight work. *Paul Leavens*

In this wonderful panoramic picture of Tonbridge, SECR D1 Class No.31470 is seen ascending Somerhill Bank with the 9.19am Sevenoaks to Hastings train on 16th June 1957. This was the last day of steam traction's monopoly of Hastings Line services, because the first batch of diesel units was introduced from the following day. Full dieselisation of the route's regular passenger services took place in June 1958. The history of the short Tonbridge to Tunbridge Wells Central line is relatively straightforward. The initial impetus for a rail connection serving the latter location came in the early 1840s after the SER had opened its line from Redhill to Tonbridge (then known as Tunbridge). The noble Marquises of Tunbridge Wells immediately recognised the advantage of a rail link to their select and fashionable town and opened negotiations with the landowners. Terms were arranged and construction commenced in 1844. The 4½ miles-long line included a substantial viaduct at Southborough and a tunnel costing £100,000. It opened to a temporary terminus at Jackwood Springs (later the site of the Tunbridge Wells goods yard) on 20th September 1845. When Wells tunnel was completed the route was extended to (what later became) Tunbridge Wells Central. At one time there was no direct connection with Tonbridge station and trains from Tunbridge Wells ran in an easterly direction for almost three-quarters of a mile along a siding on the up side of the main line. They then had to reverse into Tonbridge station. These manoeuvres were necessary for twelve years until a direct connection was installed in 1857. The original line remained *in situ*, however, and saw considerable use during World War I, but was removed shortly before the grouping in 1923. *Neil Sprinks*

In this typical scene from the early 1960s BR Standard Class 4MT 2-6-4T No.80033 is depicted climbing towards High Brooms with the 11.10am Tonbridge to Eastbourne train on a June day in 1961. The Tonbridge to Hastings line climbs quite steeply all the way from Tonbridge to just beyond Strawberry Hill tunnel, which is located between Tunbridge Wells Central and Frant. This train, however, would have diverged at Grove Junction, where the single line to Tunbridge Wells West left the 'main line'. Later the train would have traversed the outstandingly beautiful 'Cuckoo Line' to Heathfield and Polegate which was, regrettably, largely closed in June 1965. *Paul Leavens*

Tunbridge Wells Central station is a very tricky location for photography owing to its cramped, tightly-curved location in a cutting. The substantial platform awnings at the London end are an additional drawback, rendering photography on that part of the station virtually impossible. In this view, the 5.45am London Bridge to Hastings passenger train is seen awaiting departure behind Maunsell 'Schools' Class 4-4-0 No.30928 *Stowe* on 6th May 1961. By this date the bulk of the passenger trains on the Hastings line were formed of diesel units, and only a few 'odd' passenger workings remained in the hands of steam traction. The locomotive workings for 1957 reveal that the engine for this train left Bricklayers Arms shed at the unearthly hour of 3.50am and worked empty stock from Rotherhithe Road carriage sidings to Cannon Street before forming the 5.45am departure from London Bridge, which reached Hastings at 8.25am. *Chris Gammell*

In this fascinating photograph of an R Class 0-4-4T, No.31666 is seen at Tunbridge Wells West station in 1955. At first sight this locomotive could easily be mistaken for a SECR H Class, however the R Class was a Kirtley design for the LCDR which first appeared in 1891. These engines, which weighed 48tons 15cwt., were constructed for suburban services in the London area. They were successful and well-liked by enginemen, so the design was perpetuated by the SECR who built a second batch which entered traffic in 1900. These later locomotives, which were known as R1s, were totally different from the better known SER R1 Class 0-6-0Ts, which were especially associated with the Folkestone Harbour branch. The similarity of the Rs (and their sister R1s) to the H Class engines is explained by the fact that they were later fitted with H Class boilers, so many parts of the engines looked quite similar. Withdrawal of both classes commenced in the late 1940s and all had gone by the mid-1950s, long before colour photography became commonplace, so this shot must also be quite a rarity. *D. A. Kelso/Colour-Rail*

The route from Paddock Wood to Maidstone was sanctioned in 1843 and opened on 25th September 1844. It was the SER's first branch line and ran alongside the river Medway for much of the way. In 1853 an Act was obtained to extend the branch from Maidstone to Strood, this 10¾-mile link opening on 18th June 1856. Despite the secondary status of the route, the line was electrified as part of the Kent Coast stage two electrification programme in June 1961, the newly-laid conductor rails being clearly visible. In this picture SECR C Class 0-6-0 No.31716 is depicted leaving East Farleigh with a Maidstone-bound train on 18th May 1961. *Chris Gammell*

TONBRIDGE TO MAIDSTONE WEST

In this illustration, recorded at Maidstone West, SECR C Class 0-6-0 No.31244 is seen resting after arrival (and running-round) with the 5.33pm from Sevenoaks on 3rd June 1961. The locomotive is in absolutely appalling external condition. Presumably, with the official end of steam traction in Kent only a week or so away when this picture was taken, the shed staff had lost interest in maintaining their engines in respectable condition. No.31244 was built at Ashford Works in April 1902 and was withdrawn in October 1961. *Michael Allen*

By the mid-1850s two routes were available from Gravesend to London, the SER line to London Bridge and the route from Tilbury to Fenchurch Street, which was easily reached by ferry from Gravesend. Despite this, the LCDR was determined to serve the town, and fostered the nominally independent Gravesend Railway to build a five miles-long branch from Fawkham Junction, near Farningham Road. This line was incorporated in 1881 and opened on 10th May 1886. The LCDR directors hoped the branch would benefit from the development of Tilbury docks and also had high expectations of excursion traffic to Rosherville Gardens, a popular Victorian retreat served by an intermediate station. The line's service was initially ten weekday and seven Sunday trains and, predictably, a fares war broke out between the various operators. After World War I passenger traffic declined due to bus competition, but freight prospered and the line's fortunes seemed brighter when a ferry service to Rotterdam (with connecting boat trains) commenced in June 1922, this lasting until the outbreak of hostilities in 1939. Passenger traffic continued to ebb away and this operated for the last time in August 1953. Considerable freight traffic continued to use part of the route for some years afterwards. In this picture SECR C Class 0-6-0 No.31682 is seen shunting at Gravesend West on 21st November 1959. *Michael Allen*

THE GRAVESEND WEST BRANCH

A general view of Gravesend West station taken on the same day as the previous picture. Formerly known as 'Gravesend West Street', the station's name was changed in September 1949. The station was a terminus: the platform on the left was normally used by Rotterdam boat trains while local services were usually confined to the opposite platform. The boat trains to and from Victoria must have been the least pretentious of any, and were often formed of three coaches hauled by a C Class 0-6-0. Bi-lingual signs remained *in situ* long after the boat services had ceased. *Michael Allen*

GRAVESEND TO ALLHALLOWS

A branch from Gravesend (Hoo Junction) to Port Victoria, on the Isle of Grain, was proposed by the Hundred of Hoo Railway and received Parliamentary consent in 1879. This independent company was soon taken over by the SER which obtained powers for a deep water pier at Port Victoria, thus enabling the SER to compete with a steamer service from Queenborough to Flushing operated by the rival LCDR. The eleven miles-long line opened to passengers as far as Sharnal Street on 4th April 1882 and throughout on 11th September of that year. The SER had ambitious plans for Port Victoria, but the amalgamation of the LCDR and SER in 1899 (to form the SECR) removed competition, and a steady decline in boat train traffic ensued. In 1906 six halts were opened in an attempt to generate more local custom, the trains being operated by steam railmotors for a short time. In 1910 a cement works was established near Cliffe and during World War I military depots in the area brought further freight traffic to the branch, a trend which continued in subsequent years. Meanwhile the pier at Port Victoria had been declared unsafe in about 1916, traffic continued to dwindle, and in 1951 the line was cut back one mile to a new terminus at Grain to serve a new oil refinery. In 1932 a new line was constructed from Stoke Junction to Allhallows-on-Sea, which the over-optimistic Southern Railway hoped to develop as a resort. For most people, however, Allhallows was the 'last resort' and it never became a threat to the popular Kent holiday centres. Passenger receipts continued to fall and passenger trains on the entire branch ran for the last time on 3rd December 1961. Freight traffic continued to prosper on the section to Grain, serving the oil terminal which was built in the early 1950s, but the branch to Allhallows closed completely. The branch trains ran to and from Gravesend Central, and in this portrait SECR H Class No.31322 is seen waiting to leave there with an Allhallows working on 28th March 1959. *Michael Allen*

A view of Sharnal Street with H Class No.31553 propelling a Gravesend to Allhallows train out of the station. This photograph was taken on 22nd May 1961. The station's isolated, rural location is evident in the picture. It was intended to serve the village of Hoo, but this was located over two miles away, so the station is unlikely to have been busy. In 1901 a standard-gauge line was opened from Sharnal Street to ammunition stores at Lodge Hill, the line being later extended to Chattenden where it connected with the 2ft 6in gauge Chattenden & Upnor Railway. The standard-gauge line was known as the Chattenden Naval Tramway, and in 1901 this was extended southwards to Kingsnorth Pier. There were exchange sidings at Sharnal Street, which became a relatively important freight traffic centre for a time. All of these lines had been closed by the early 1960s. *David Clark*

Photographed in glorious winter sunshine, H Class No.31517 is seen at Sharnal Street on 9th January 1960. Initially six local trains were provided on weekdays to Port Victoria, plus two boat trains in connection with sailings to Belgium. When the Allhallows branch opened in 1932 the service was more than doubled to thirteen trains per day, some of which included through carriages to and from London. Port Victoria's service was reduced to two 'rush-hour only' weekday trains. A remarkably generous service of thirteen weekday trains continued to be timetabled right up to closure, despite the unremunerative nature of the route. *Chris Gammell*

‘You have been warned’, trespass on the railway at your peril! These lineside notices were photographed between Middle Stoke Halt and Stoke Junction Halt on 8th November 1961. *Michael Allen*

Unlike the middle and western end of the Hoo Peninsula, where the land rises to just over 200ft. above sea level, the area around Allhallows is largely flat. In this view an unidentified H Class engine approaches Allhallows-on-Sea station with a train from Gravesend, across an empty landscape where the station's water tower is the most prominent landmark. Construction of this 1¾ mile long branch commenced in August 1929 and the first excursion arrived on 14th May 1932. Only a modest single platform station was built at first, but a second platform was commissioned in April 1933 (creating a platform with tracks on each side) and a longer canopy provided, this being in the pleasing Southern Railway style of the period. The line was doubled in the mid-1930s, but reverted to single track once again in 1957. Despite the enterprise displayed by the SR, the population of Allhallows increased by only 250 persons between 1930 and 1960, so their efforts totally failed. The final train, hauled by filthy SECR C Class 0-6-0 No.31689, left Allhallows at 8.38pm on 3rd December 1961 and this little-known branch, which had a life of less than 30 years, faded into history. *Ken Wightman*

The seven miles-long branch from Sittingbourne to Sheerness, on the Isle of Sheppey, was opened by an independent company on 19th July 1860, but the line was taken over by the LCDR six years later. The branch made a triangular junction with the main Chatham to Faversham line half a mile west of Sittingbourne station. The line was constructed as a single-track route, but was doubled as far as Swale Halt in 1959 as part of the improvements associated with the Kent Coast electrification. In this photograph LMSR-designed Ivatt Class 2MT 2-6-2T No.41300 is seen leaving the intermediate station of Queenborough on 13th June 1959. The coaches are a BR Standard 3-set in carmine and cream livery. Queenborough Pier, reached by a short branch line, was once the start of steamer services to Flushing, for which connecting boat trains ran from Victoria. The ferry services had largely ceased by the 1920s, as a result of Dover's increasing importance as a cross-Channel port. Most of the track to the pier had been removed by the late 1950s. *R. C. Riley*

SITTINGBOURNE TO SHEERNESS

The principal point of interest on the otherwise unspectacular Sheerness branch is the crossing of the river Swale, a narrow stretch of water which separated the Isle of Sheppey from the mainland. Here, SECR C Class 0-6-0 No.31495 is illustrated crossing the old bridge with the 1.22pm Sheerness to Sittingbourne train in June 1959. The old King's Ferry bridge, which dated from 1904, incorporated a rolling lift span which necessitated a weight restriction, and it was also prone to damage by passing ships. In 1960 it was replaced by a new vertical lift structure which is under construction in the background, completely dwarfing the train. *G. H. Hunt/Colour-Rail*

THE HAWKHURST BRANCH

Various proposals were put forward in the 1840s for lines across the Weald of Kent linking Paddock Wood or Headcorn and Rye but nothing came of these. In 1864, however, a local company obtained powers for a branch from Paddock Wood to Cranbrook and another concern proposed an ambitious extension to Tenterden. These ideas were killed off by a banking collapse in 1866, which made funds much more difficult to obtain, and matters rested until 1877 when the Cranbrook & Paddock Wood Railway Company was incorporated. The company also found it hard to attract money, and little progress was made until the SER became involved. Work began in earnest in 1891 and on 1st October 1892 the line opened to Hope Mill (later Goudhurst). It was opened throughout to Hawkhurst on 4th September 1893. In many ways the steeply-graded Hawkhurst branch was the most attractive in Kent, threading its way through the 'garden of England' past some of the county's most productive apple orchards and hop gardens. This view of a Locomotive Club of Great Britain 'last day' railtour was taken between Paddock Wood and Horsmonden, with two 0-6-0s in charge. Both locomotives – O1 Class No.31065 and C Class No.31592 – are preserved on the Bluebell Railway. *Paul Leavens*

Horsmonden station, located almost 4½ miles from Paddock Wood, was the summit of a steep 1 in 66 climb for southbound trains and many a hop-pickers' special, which were much heavier trains than the branch's regular two-coach push-pull formations, has come to grief on the bank due to shortage of steam. SECR H Class 0-4-4T No.31324 is seen posing with the 2.15pm Paddock Wood to Hawkhurst train on 3rd June 1961. The station building consists of a simple single-storey structure of corrugated iron with a short platform awning. There was a two-road goods yard here, on the up side, while on the down side was a siding in the form of a loop. The latter enabled Horsmonden station to cross trains, but it was unable to cross two local passenger trains because the station had only one platform. During the season a local fruit packing factory used to send wagon-loads of apples to destinations as distant as Aberdeen. *Michael Allen*

After leaving Horsmonden the line ran along the valley of the river Teise, passing more hop gardens on the slopes of the nearby Wealden Hills. Two miles further on, Goudhurst station was reached, where there was a fully signalled passing loop and two platforms. Like so many branch line stations in Great Britain it was inconveniently positioned for the village, which was 300 feet higher than the station, a tough proposition for a passenger not being met by a car. No.31324 is seen again, this time with the 4.25pm from Paddock Wood on the same date as the previous shot. *Michael Allen*

A further view of Goudhurst station showing the substantially built stationmaster's house on the up platform, which was quite an impressive structure compared to the meagre buildings provided at some other stations on the line. No.31324 is seen once more, this time propelling a Paddock Wood-bound train on 6th May 1961. *Dennis Ovenden*

Shunt signals do not come much daintier than this! This fascinating piece of SECR signalling equipment was photographed at Goudhurst on 3rd June 1961. *Michael Allen*

Hawkhurst station, 11½ miles from Paddock Wood, had a single platform with a short bay and a run-round loop long enough for six coaches. The goods yard had three sidings and a long-disused engine shed. The station building was extremely modest, consisting only of corrugated iron structures. There was a fine view over Romney Marsh from the station, which was at an altitude of 200 feet above sea level, but this was probably of less interest to travellers than its location, a mile away from the village across a wide valley. The picturesque Hawkhurst branch had a long association with hop pickers' specials, which started running from London to the Kentish hopfields in the 19th century. During late August and early September of each year hundreds of families, commonly known as 'hoppers', would travel in special trains from the grimy working-class suburbs of south-east London for a working, paid holiday in the invigorating fresh air of the Kent countryside. During the 1950s higher living standards, coupled with increasing machine picking, steadily reduced this traffic, the Hawkhurst branch seeing its last through hop pickers' train in 1959. Due to the very short shunting neck at Hawkhurst, 4-4-0s and 0-6-0s were the largest engines permitted on the branch, so the operation of these trains was always of particular interest to railway enthusiasts. The branch usually suffered from poor connections with London trains at Paddock Wood and, as already mentioned, the stations were often badly sited in relation to the villages they purported to serve. Towards the end, many of the regular passengers were schoolchildren, but this vital traffic was lost to buses in about 1958, a blow from which the branch never recovered. It is unlikely that the line ever made a profit, and the inevitable closure took place in June 1961. *Michael Allen*

ASHFORD TO HASTINGS

In 1845 the Brighton, Lewes & Hastings Railway Company sought parliamentary powers for an extension from St. Leonards through Hastings and Rye to Ashford, where a junction with the SER was projected. The SER countered with proposals for a branch from Headcorn to Hastings, but Parliament, and more especially the Duke of Wellington, was anxious to have a railway available to carry troops along the extremely vulnerable stretch of coastline near the proposed Hastings and Ashford line. A decision was made in favour of the coastal scheme and, in addition, Parliament stipulated that the line should be built and operated by the SER. Despite the easy nature of the route, the 28 mile long line took some time to construct, and was not opened until 13th February 1851. Intermediate stations were initially provided at Ham Street, Appledore, Rye and Winchelsea. Some of the line's stations were designed by William Tress in the Italianate style and these included Appledore, seen here on 14th June 1964. The building was originally built on symmetrical lines, the small extension, on the left, presumably being a later addition. The modern signal box, which controlled the level crossing, is prominent on the left of the picture. *Michael Allen*

'Appledore for Lydd & New Romney Branch' proclaims the running-in board on Appledore's westbound platform. Unfortunately, it is no longer a passenger junction, the service to New Romney having been withdrawn from 6th March 1967, but the track remains *in situ* across the bleak and featureless marshland as far as Dungeness for the transport of waste from the nuclear power station. Like so many rural stations Appledore suffers from its poor location, over a mile from the village it purports to serve but, as the saying goes, 'they had to build the station next to the railway line'. *Michael Allen*

Diesel multiple units started to replace steam engines on the Hastings to Ashford line from about 1957 and by the summer of 1959 steam traction on passenger workings was almost a thing of the past. One or two steam passenger duties survived long after this time, however, notably the 8.34am (weekdays) Hastings to Ashford and the 6.50am from Hastings on a Sunday morning. Remarkably, the latter working was booked to be hauled by a Maunsell 'Schools' Class 4-4-0, a type which had been prohibited from the line until the 1950s due to weight restrictions. In this quite rare colour picture of steam traction at work on the line in ordinary service, No.30928 *Stowe* is depicted pausing at Ham Street & Orlestone station on the sunny morning of 21st May 1961. Luckily, the photographer lived locally at the time and was therefore able to obtain this especially interesting shot. *Dennis Ovenden*

THE FOLKESTONE HARBOUR BRANCH

The Folkestone Harbour branch is different from other branch lines in Kent, because it was built principally to convey international boat train traffic, and not for local passengers. There was not even a direct connection with the main line at Folkestone Junction (later known as Folkestone East). The SER purchased the harbour, which was in a neglected condition, in 1843, and construction of the harbour branch commenced during the same year. The branch was opened to passenger traffic from 1st January 1849. Meanwhile in 1845 the SER had formed a subsidiary company to operate steamers from Folkestone and Dover to Calais, Boulogne and Ostend. Improvements to the harbour were undertaken in 1863, when a new pier was built into deeper water, this being extended in 1885 to enable a fixed timetable of sailings to be operated independently of the tides. For many years trains on the branch were powered by R1 Class 0-6-0Ts, four of which are seen in this picture, taken in dramatic lighting conditions, at Folkestone Junction on 31st January 1959. *Chris Gammell*

The Folkestone Harbour branch is best known for its exceptionally steep 1 in 30 gradient which London-bound trains have to tackle immediately after departure from the harbour station. Unfortunately, there was no opportunity for enginemen to take a 'run' at the bank; all they could do was to ensure boiler pressure was high and then keep their fingers crossed during the battle ahead! Over the years proposals have been made for alternative approaches to the harbour, most notably by extending the line from Sandling Junction to Hythe and Sandgate along the coast, but this was opposed by the townspeople and local landowners. So, until electrification in 1961, the branch provided one of the most magnificent displays of the raw power of steam traction in southern England, as very heavy boat trains were heaved up the incline by up to three R1 Class locomotives. Nearby houses must have been shaken to their foundations as the trains passed by! Here, a pair of R1s is seen blasting up the gradient towards Folkestone Junction with a Stephenson Locomotive Society railtour on 19th May 1957. The picture was taken from Radnor Bridge Road which crosses over the line at this point, the harbour station being just out of sight around the bend. *Neil Sprinks*

In contrast to the previous shot, in this much more tranquil scene an R1 Class 0-6-0T is depicted easing a train across the bridge towards Folkestone Harbour station, also on 19th May 1957. The start of the gradient towards the main line is clearly visible. The line crossed the harbour on a series of brick arches and a swing bridge and divided the inner harbour (on the left) from the outer harbour. In the nineteenth century the local landowners, the Earls of Radnor, recognised the potential of the attractive environment offered by the cliffs above the harbour. They created a high class resort with large villas and hotels while other entertainment amenities were established. The SER was slow to develop this new source of traffic, but in 1896 a Pullman-style luxury train was introduced between London and Folkestone only. After the First World War expresses from Charing Cross were speeded-up to run the 70 miles to Folkestone in 80 minutes. *Neil Sprinks*

An R1 Class 0-6-0T locomotive, No.31047, is seen shunting the carriage sidings at Folkestone Harbour in 1954. There was a large layout there, which extended along the pier towards the lighthouse. This included thirteen sidings and a goods warehouse east of the station, rail access to which was obtained by running onto the pier and then reversing into the goods yard. The carriage sidings were located on the west side of the line and, once again, trains had to reverse into the sidings after passing through the station. This bank of sidings was sandwiched between the seashore and Marine Parade. The hotels in the immediate area doubtless offered excellent vantage points from where any visiting rail enthusiasts could observe activity at the station and sidings, although it is likely other snootier guests may not have been quite as appreciative of the view from their rooms! Both the coaches visible are Maunsell-designed 'nondescript' brake vehicles dating from the early 1930s, the term 'nondescript' indicating a coach that could be used for any class of travel, depending on the circumstances. Generally, these unusual vehicles were classified 'second' for boat train traffic, although the seating arrangement (two on one side of the central aisle and one on the other) was virtually to first class standard. Since this picture was taken, much of the rail infrastructure at Folkestone Harbour has been dramatically reduced and these sidings have long since disappeared, also some of the buildings in the shot have been demolished. The goods facilities were withdrawn in August 1968 and all the associated tracks were subsequently removed. *Colour-Rail*